A NEW MINDSET FOR COUNTERING TERRORISM

Nothing has shaped the security environment of the 21st century more than the specter of global terrorism. As the sole remaining superpower, how the United States responds to, and can affect terrorism will have a profound impact on world security for decades to come. This paper examines U.S. counterterrorism policy, national security interests and foreign relations to establish options for a more effective policy that provides a national direction and synchronizes all instruments of national power in the struggle against terrorism. For the purpose of this paper, I will analyze terrorism in the context of transnational movements rather than individual acts or organizations. A new mindset is necessary to accurately analyze the threat and craft a successful vision that leads to a more effective policy, not only to combat terrorism in the near term, but to ultimately protect U.S. interests domestically and abroad in the long-term.

The Road to Current Policy

American policy and actions in the past several decades are a legacy that the rest of the world is keenly observing and devising strategies against. In the post-World War II era, terrorism was a tactic commonly used by militant groups as a violent means to bring about political change within their ruling governments. As a stable democracy, the United States was largely immune to the influence of terrorism, particularly to the homeland during this period. Moreover, the U.S. was engaged in a monolithic struggle against communism in the Cold War; counterterrorism received little attention in the realm of National Security Strategy. Although President Reagan first established a Combating Terrorism Task Force with National Security Decision Directive 179 (NSDD-179),[1] it focused primarily on travel of U.S. citizens abroad and the security of service members. It was not until the Clinton Administration when international terrorism became considered a significant national security threat.

Clinton Administration, 1992-2000

The most significant occurrences of international terrorism against U.S. interests prior to the Clinton administration were the Beirut bombing in 1983, the Achille Lauro hijacking in 1985, and the Pan Am flight 103 bombing in Lockerbie, Scotland.[2] These attacks characterized international terrorism at the time, which was motivated by a desire to influence policy, exploit Palestinian unrest, anti-Zionism and increase the influence of groups such as Hezbollah and the Palestinian Liberation Organization (PLO). Additionally, state sponsors of terrorism like Libya fomented anti-Western sentiment in the Middle East, yet lacked the audacity or the means to attack the U.S. homeland. Thus, the rise of international terrorism in the 1970s and 1980s caused a sense of vulnerability for Americans abroad, but also reinforced a sense of security that the U.S. homeland was insulated from terrorist attacks.

In 1993, the Al Qaeda bombing of the World Trade Center exposed a vulnerability to terrorist attacks on U.S. soil, in addition to revealing an increased audacity and determination of international terrorist networks. In 1995, the Clinton Administration issued a Presidential Decision Directive outlining *U.S. Policy on Counterterrorism*, entitled PDD-39. The directive outlined four basic elements for combating terrorism: reduce vulnerabilities; deter; respond; and weapons of mass destruction. It also stated the intent to deter, defeat and respond vigorously to preempt, apprehend and prosecute governments or individuals that perpetrate or plan such attacks. The directive further reiterated that U.S. policy will not be affected by terrorist acts. [3] The counterterrorism policy announced in PDD-39 was largely focused on

2

defense and deterrence, relying heavily on diplomacy, sanctions and increased vigilance. A fairly comprehensive policy, it emphasized passive and reactive measures with the offensive focus tied primarily to preventing the acquisition and use of weapons of mass destruction.

Bush Administration, 2000-2008

The attacks of September 11, 2001, provided the basis for the Bush administration counterterrorism policy. The brazen re-attacks by Al Qaeda on U.S. soil caused rapid and substantive changes to U.S. counterterrorism policy and foreign relations. The Bush administration formed the Department of Homeland Security (DHS) as a cabinet level office charged as lead agency for protecting the territory of the U.S. from terrorist attacks, while the State Department and Department of Defense retained responsibilities abroad.[4]

Although there have been no successful terrorist attacks against the U.S. homeland since 9-11, a heavy cost in blood and treasure has been expended in the subsequent wars in Afghanistan and Iraq. Each conflict sought and achieved regime changes to protect the U.S. from future terrorist attacks, but have expanded into drawn out insurgencies that have inspired greater resentment against the West and injected substantial financial and physical support for terrorist organizations and ideologies like Al Qaeda and the Taliban. Regime change in and of itself failed to deter, and may, in fact, have contributed to the expansion of terrorism.

A significant outcome of the Bush years was that a widespread perception developed that viewed terrorism as a struggle between radical Muslims against the Western world. In some circles, U.S. policy came to be viewed as a war against Islam.

3

This distortion was fueled by the conflict being dubbed "The Global War on Terror," (GWOT), and the U.S. determination to hunt terrorists to the ends of the earth also had a polarizing effect that was exploited by radicals. Another damaging foreign policy blow to the U.S. was President Bush"s 2002 State of the Union Address which named Iran, Iraq and North Korea as part of an "Axis of Evil". It sent a message that the U.S. was not looking to negotiate and consequently resulted in the invasion of Iraq and ignited urgency in nuclear weapon development by Iran and North Korea.[5] This new course was formally articulated in the 2002 National Security Strategy which introduced two key policy principles of unilateralism and preemption, which came to be known as the "Bush Doctrine."[6] These actions started reversing the groundswell of support the U.S. enjoyed after 9-11. The policy actions of the U.S. divided domestic and world opinion, while implying a message about U.S. intentions to unilaterally prosecute the "GWOT" against an enemy broader than just Al Qaeda.

Obama Administration, 2008 to Present

The Obama administration has yet to introduce a formal counterterrorism policy, instead continuing generally along existing policy lines; however, the administration has made significant changes in the strategies of the wars in Iraq and Afghanistan. The administration accepted responsibility for two wars mired in insurgency, struggling to rebuild infrastructure and establish democracy where it had not existed before. They made clear a desire to rapidly draw down U.S. forces in Iraq to divert resources toward Afghanistan, which they viewed as the "just war" and harbored those responsible for 9-11. In outlining his strategy for Afghanistan, President Obama moved away from nation building and redefined the U.S. objectives in Afghanistan to: 1) deny Al Qaeda safe haven, 2) reverse Taliban momentum and deny the ability to overthrow the government, and 3) strengthen the Afghan government and security forces.[7] In essence, the early actions of the Obama administration moved U.S. policy away from a GWOT, narrowed military objectives and expressed a desire to extricate from the conflict in order to concentrate on domestic issues. These changes are counter to previous policy to take the fight to the enemy, dismantle terrorist regimes and hunt terrorists relentlessly throughout the world; moreover, it moved toward repairing the U.S. image and foreign relations.

Over the past few decades, U.S. counterterrorism policy has been inconsistent; shifting between what critics might view as bureaucratic and soft, to a neo-imperialist imposition of western values, to an ambiguous mix of conciliation and waning resolve. When Afghanistan and Iraq transitioned from wars of liberation to insurgencies, the U.S. failed to adjust their national objectives in accordance with the new paradigm, instead adapting strategies to defeat the latest perceived threat. This incoherence is reflective of the counterterrorism policy trend over the years.

As the sole superpower, the U.S. wears a bull"s-eye on its back and will face challenges by state and non-state actors. Is terrorism something that can be defeated through war in the same way an invading nation might be militarily conquered? That is a question that must be examined as the current war enters a second decade with no discernible end in sight. A clear understanding of the threat is necessary to build a solid and consistent policy along with an effective strategy that transcends administrations and denies terrorists their objectives.

Objective of Policy and Strategy

U.S. counterterrorism policy should define clear goals and represent the national interest. The corresponding strategy cannot simply be a reflection of a desire to preserve those interests, such as protecting democracy and self-determination. An effective strategy must obtain national interests, and therefore, must effectively overcome the threat. With the uncertain nature of the threat, the proliferation of weapons of mass destruction, and the distinction of being the most prominent symbol of anti-western enmity, it is well within the United States security interest to reserve the right to preempt and/or retaliate toward any aggressor that threatens American citizens or U.S. interests. This caveat is necessary due to the threat, but as a matter of policy, it should not be construed as an automatic declaration of war, but more as an instrument to eradicate threats based on prioritized interests. This is significant because some practitioners of global jihad have the expressed goal of attacking the United States simply to invite a war with the West.[8] This is the dichotomy of "fighting" terrorism; terror is a tactic and countering that tactic with the use of force often strengthens the cause of the terrorist. A well crafted U.S. policy and strategy should go beyond defeating the tactic, but address the root causes that inspire the use of that tactic, are consistent with the rule of law, and are more compelling than the radical alternatives espoused by terrorist ideologies and organizations.

Clarify the Terminology

To develop an effective strategy, one must understand and clarify the terminology. This task is complicated, since there is no universally agreed upon definition of terrorism and it is unlikely that a consensus will ever be reached due to the significant nuances and implications a collective definition might generate. This illustrates why understanding terrorism is so problematic. If the very definition has multiple and varied interpretations, imagine the myriad of potential solutions the variously interpreted definitions might inspire. Expanding this concept, it is instructive to examine how organizations representing the instruments of national power define terrorism.

Diplomatically, the U.S. State Department defines terrorism as, "a premeditated, politically motivated violence perpetrated against noncombatant targets by subnational groups or clandestine agents, usually intended to influence an audience. "[9] Militarily, Department of Defense defines terrorism as, "the calculated use of unlawful violence or threat of unlawful violence to inculcate fear; intended to coerce or to intimidate governments or societies in the pursuit of goals that are generally political, religious, or ideological." [10]

In the Information realm, the United Nations has been unable to reach a consensus on defining terrorism primarily due to the standoff with the Organization of the Islamic Conference (OIC). The OIC seeks to insert into the Convention,

> "The activities of the parties during an armed conflict, including in situations of foreign occupation....are not governed by this Convention." Or, as the Pakistani delegate describes the standoff on behalf of the OIC, there is a need "to make a distinction between terrorism and the exercise of legitimate right of peoples to resist foreign occupation." This claim purports to exclude blowing up certain civilians from the reach of international law and organizations. It is central to interpreting every proclamation by the states which have ratified these conventions in any UN forum purporting to combat terrorism.[11]

Some would argue that one man"s terrorist is another man"s freedom fighter. It is the inherent right of societies to defend themselves against invaders; however, attacks on civilians clearly violate norms protecting non-combatants and cannot be justified.

Although not authoritatively recognized, but valuable in the context of this discussion; a November 2004 United Nations Secretary General report described terrorism as any act "intended to cause death or serious bodily harm to civilians or non-combatants with the purpose of intimidating a population or compelling a government or an international organization to do or abstain from doing any act"."[12]

Clearly, terrorism is difficult to define and its elusive character has led to a basic misunderstanding of the concept. Many definitions are in agreement that the **means** of terrorism are manifested through violence in order to influence a desired outcome or **endstate**. What is debatable is the **ways** of terrorism; or what is the distinction between an act of war, an act of terror, or the commission of a crime. Is this violence legitimate expression of self-determination? Can one define combatants and non-combatants in this type of struggle? Those answers go beyond the scope of this paper, but they underscore the implications of building a strategy based on an imprecise understanding of what terrorism is, and what it is not. In some instances, the terminology and concepts converge. I will use the terms extremist, radical Islamist, jihadist and terrorist interchangeably because they all share the same characteristic of attacking and instilling fear upon non-combatants.

Implications of a "War on Terror"

Consider the following: conventional warfare employs violence as a means to an end but the ways are determined by leaders, whereas terrorism is the infliction of fear and violence as the ways that all means will be brought to bear to achieve the ends. Therefore, *inflicting terror itself is a component of the desired endstate*, regardless of other considerations such as non-combatant status. Terrorism is a fear inspiring tactic that must be countered, not an enemy that one might defeat with force. Of the numerous definitions of war, the majority contain specific elements such as identifying the belligerents, the use of arms or violence, and an overall purpose or objective. For example, a typical encyclopedia definition of war explains it as,

> " armed conflict between states or nations (international war) or between factions within a state (civil war), prosecuted by force and having the purpose of compelling the defeated side to do the will of the victor. Among the causes of war are ideological, political, racial, economic, and religious conflicts." [13]

The use of the word "war" in reference to a war on terror rather than a chosen enemy is essentially metaphorical to underline a resolve and rejection of any type of acquiescence. It expresses a conviction that terrorism is as destructive as war and the resolve to fight those responsible no less than wartime enemies. This has become problematic because the use of the word "war" has gone far beyond metaphor to acquire a strategic reality.[14] The issue with automatically identifying terrorism with war is multi-fold. First, terrorism is not an enemy, it is a tactic. Second, the use of the term "war," legitimizes terrorists. It also allows them to conjure images of the crusades and colonialism. It permits radicals to twist Western actions into a war against Islam. An additional problem with the term "war" is that it is a reciprocal process: if you are at war with someone, then he is at war with you. As a result, the state of war confers a degree of common dignity on the belligerents, as well as certain rights, even if the belligerents do not abide by those rights.[15] Recognizing terror as a tactic, it then remains that an enemy must be identified. The Bush and Obama administrations, while fighting simultaneous insurgencies, struggled with specifically defining the "terrorist" enemy. The enemy has grown from Al Qaeda, Hezbollah, Hamas, Iraqi insurgents, Taliban, radicals in Pakistan and others to become subsumed into a single monolithic entity.[16] Unfortunately, this afforded great latitude for others to dictate who the enemy is, or more significantly to cloud what, or who the true enemy is. Al Qaeda presents the greatest transnational terrorist threat to U.S. interests in the near term, but rather than identifying a particular movement, the War on Terror was expanded beyond Al Qaeda. By portraying the enemy in the context of global terrorism, the perception served to coalesce Islamic extremism writ large as a unified adversary, when previously it had been marked more by its schisms than its unity.

By properly identifying the enemy, one is better able to devise strategies to defeat that enemy; whereas, strategies to defeat a tactic will only alter the tactics and fail to produce a true endstate. The adversary will adapt but will not be defeated. By defeating the adversary, the tactic is rendered useless. In the sense that most western thinkers define war, end goals and aims constitute another dimension when dealing with terrorism. In the Westphalian system, states employ diplomacy or force to effect political or economic change. This is not necessarily true for all terrorist groups, whereas terrorism is not the means to the end, but the end in itself.[17]

A major distinction to be made in the discussion of warfare is to address a fundamental misunderstanding and intermingling of terms such as guerilla warfare, insurgency, irregular warfare and terrorism. Insurgencies and guerilla wars are fought to achieve political objectives. Although their tactics may include unconventional warfare or terrorism, the use of force is the means to achieve political ends and asymmetric methods or terror are ways that an insurgent force or guerilla army might bring that force to bear. The ways and the means are not necessarily one in the same.

The confusion surrounding terrorism is exacerbated because activities we commonly associate with terrorism appear to bear many similarities with the forms of guerilla warfare. Such activities may, for the political actor who employs such tactics, possess many of the same objectives such as aiming to force the adversary to negotiate favorable terms.[18] It is also true that terrorism can form an adjunct to a number of so called unconventional practices of war. Yet there are distinct differences between guerilla warfare and terrorism, and it is important not to describe all insurgency warfare as terrorist in character.[19] As terminology and concepts are convoluted, the most significant nuances are lost. For instance, one might wage war against an insurgent group or a guerrilla army and deny their aims by militarily defeating their forces or negotiating a truce, in effect achieving victory. However, a war waged on terror defines the adversary by the tactic, distances strategy from objectives and distorts the focus from defeat of the enemy to extinguishing an ideology. State support for jihadist groups such as Al Qaeda has essentially vanished. Rather than maintain territorial sanctuaries, such groups have melted away into their host societies to a point where "war" is both infeasible in practice and analytically misleading.[20] Within this framework, policy and strategy are unlikely to produce decisive victory when there is no military center of gravity to mass forces against and there is no distinguishable disposition of forces to be attacked.[21]

The basic argument for containment is twofold. First, a war on terror is misguided and is more a reaction to the environment rather than an effort toward shaping the future environment. Policy should ensure that strategy pursues appropriate aims, while strategy informs policy of the art of the possible.[22] Second, if the national interest and objectives are to combat terrorism, their achievement requires using all instruments of national power, guided by the direction of a clear policy supported by a grand strategy to meet the national aims. This includes the use of force where appropriate, but force is best directed against a tangible enemy rather than ambiguously defined threats. Force alone has negligible impact against ideology, but the combined effect of national power has the capability to contain large-scale movements.

Declaring terror as an enemy creates frustrating non-sequiturs, but it also obfuscates a fundamental understanding that must be achieved prior to embarking upon war. Political and military leaders must understand the type of war they are fighting. As Carl Von Clausewitz said,

> "The first, the supreme, the most far-reaching act of judgment that the statesman and commander have to make is to establish by that test the kind of war on which they are embarking; neither mistaking it for, nor trying to turn it into, something that is alien to its nature. This is the first of all strategic questions and the most comprehensive." [23]

It is in this endeavor that the U.S. would have been wise to consider the implications of waging war against a tactic that is so complex that it defies common definition, so widespread that it inspires enemies and sympathizers to multiply and splinter into indiscriminate factions, and so ambiguous that neither the enemy nor the battlefield is readily discernible. In this type of fight, defeat is much more measurable than victory.

Reshaping the Understanding of the Problem

It has taken years to recognize the power of the words that built policy, but it appears that the U.S. leadership is realizing that a new mindset is necessary to combat terrorism. In March of 2009, the Obama administration announced that the term "Global War on Terror" would be dropped in lieu of "Overseas Contingency Operations." [24] This

12

announcement was made with little fanfare, but it punctuated a notable shift that began late in the Bush administration from the terminology that critics claimed, including some within the U.S. military, mischaracterized the nature of the enemy and its abilities. For example, some military officers said that classifying Al Qaeda and other anti-American militant groups as part of a single movement overstated their strength. John A. Nagl, the former Army officer who helped write the military's latest counterinsurgency field manual, criticized the term "war on terror" when he said it:

> "was enormously unfortunate because I think it pulled together disparate organizations and insurgencies. Our strategy should be to divide and conquer rather than make of enemies more than they are. We are facing a number of different insurgencies around the globe -- some have local causes, some of them are transnational. Viewing them all through one lens distorts the picture and magnifies the enemy." [25]

Nagl"s point is insightful; however, not all insurgencies are terrorist in nature and not all terrorism is the result of insurgency. Unfortunately, the two protracted insurgencies in the Middle East have created a myopia that blurs this distinction, while radical Islamism requires a much broader discussion than simply a collection of insurgencies. The significant difference between an insurgency and a terror campaign is that terrorist tactics are applied to non-combatants.

If not through a war on terror, then how might the U.S. effectively combat terrorism and achieve national security objectives? Clearly identifying and understanding the problem is a good first step and secondly it is necessary to fully understand the threat. Nations have been increasingly preoccupied with devising strategies to defeat terrorism. Where these strategies fall short is that they focus on the symptom vice the cause of terrorism; that is, they are transfixed on the violence. In some ways, these strategies are well founded and practical. By many definitions,

13

terrorism is a crime, and commission of a crime invites justice upon the perpetrator. Retaliation and use of force has a significant deterrent effect against those that would take human life and inflict severe mental distress on those deemed to be "innocent."[26] But again, it addresses only the symptom. For many, this introduces the intrinsic ethical dimension to terrorism which raises questions relating to concepts like "Just War," and non-combatant immunity, but from which a source of much debate and definitional difficulty arises.[27] The threat of, or the actual use of force is a valuable tool in the arsenal to combat terror, but it is not the only one. Effective instruments against terrorism address root causes, not just the symptoms.

Determining the Underlying Causes

Terrorists are generally driven to commit acts of terrorism due to a variety of factors, whether rational or irrational, in which extreme forms of violence are used to express specific grievances and demands. Root causes are the factors and circumstances underlying movements that radicalize and drive terrorists into carrying out violent actions.[28] One underlying cause is the people"s struggle against a corrupt or oppressive government. This generally involves non-state actors seeking to achieve their political aims primarily through terrorist violence. The wars in Iraq and Afghanistan began as operations to remove repressive regimes and were generally well received by the population initially. However, the formation of new regimes did little to improve the basic condition of the battered societies. The inability of new governments to ameliorate grievances and provide security and basic services enabled radicals to exploit social dissatisfaction within the transforming environment and shift momentum against the U.S. Meanwhile, groups mobilized resistance against the new governments and security forces utilizing a common tactic of a weaker force versus the stronger – terrorism. The removal of the Taliban and Saddam Hussein regimes failed to address the underlying societal needs, but rather, exposed the condition of marginalized people responding to ideologies that promise deliverance from their miserable circumstance.

Misreading the environment is understandable given the complexities involved, but successful policy is dependent on sorting through those complexities to get it right. The environment has an unforgiving propensity to penalize bad reads. Afghanistan and Iraq are instances where terrorist tactics and insurgency tend to be incorrectly homogenized because the fight is characterized by conventional and unconventional forces versus embattled governments engaged in a counterinsurgency campaign. Strategist Colin Gray observed a similar trend with the Vietnam War,

> "the U.S. strategy bore the hallmarks of counter-insurgency faddism that was naively captivated by the „cult of the guerrilla" and the aura of Special Forces. The resulting preoccupation with military technique came at the expense of the acute appreciation of the social and political conditions stoking the violence, causing, in particular, the weakness and corruption of the South Vietnamese state to be overlooked and the populist appeal of the elements of the Vietnamese communist message to be misunderstood." [29]

In other words, the military and the policy makers misread the environment in Vietnam, and therefore, did not understand the problem. The lack of attention to the political and social conditions led policies and strategies to be built on flawed assumptions designed to curtail the violence or protect the population but did little to strike at the basic motivation of the adversary or their networks.

Examination of the social condition in the Middle East reveals strong doubts that the United States and to some extent, Europe, is serious about democracy in Muslim countries. Western influence has been undermined by what is perceived to be a double standard in promoting democracy. The U.S. and many of its allies have a long record of supporting authoritarian regimes and failing to produce democracy in the Muslim world as they did in other regions after the fall of the Soviet Union. As former Ambassador Richard Hass acknowledged in a speech on December 4, 2002, "the U.S. government has for decades practiced "democratic exceptionalism" in the Muslim world, subordinating democracy to other U.S. interests such as accessing oil, containing the Soviet Union, and grappling with the Arab-Israeli conflict." [30]

Without overstating the case, democratic exceptionalism disadvantages the U.S. as it wages an opposing battle for the hearts and minds of Muslim people courted by the radical extremists that tap an overwhelming source of moral and spiritual support from marginalized sectors of the Middle East. In this context, it is important to distinguish that while we face a global transnational extremist movement, it is one that is often triggered and fed by local conditions and difficulties that have little to do with the West. By failing to appreciate this point, we are likely to focus unduly on the idea of an all-embracing Islamic identity shared by our adversaries that would miss the nuances of their sectarian, ethnic, linguistic or tribal identities and differences.[31] Widespread disenchantment in the Middle East does not cause terrorism, but it provides fertile ground for terrorist actors to radicalize, recruit, seek funding and operate.

American intervention in the Middle East has stoked tremendous resentment and inspired Muslims to take arms in a sacred cause to battle Western occupation of the Holy Land. This conflict has given rise to a view that violence is the only language the terrorist understands. However, meeting force with force is problematic when the objective of the terrorist is to perpetuate violence as a means to achieve their aims. Al

Qaeda mastermind Abu Musab al-Suri noted that the jihadi movement has metastasized into a self-sustaining movement in which battles and bombings are more important as a means for recruiting and radicalizing a new generation of followers than as a means to a political end.[32] This underscores the impact of using religion to radicalize and incite violence. Throughout history close ties between religion and politics have existed in societies and leaders have used religion to recruit members, to justify their actions, and to glorify fighting and dying in a sacred struggle.[33] Separating religion from violence is an essential component to a solution.

The debate about the centrality of religion to radical Islamist ideology reveals that while religion is an important motivator in the radicalization process,

> "it is also being used to legitimate a very specific worldview that has been shaped by many factors external to Islam, such as a general sense of anger and humiliation (which radicals can tap into) in reaction to events of foreign origin over which they have no control. At the same time, domestic problems in Egypt, Saudi Arabia and other Muslim countries can feed that dissatisfaction and engender support for radicalism."[34]

Objectives and Strategy of a Terrorist Movement

The most significant transnational terrorist threats today are intertwined with Islamic extremism. The rationale of Islamic extremism is often viewed too narrowly as a religious movement, but it goes beyond that. Islamic extremists seek power, social change, control over laws and the authority to dictate how society will conduct itself. Islamic extremism manifests itself in the form of Jihad or "struggle". Although the term has been corrupted from its original context that describes the struggle to be a good Muslim, the concept of Jihad is a coalescing factor that extremists leverage to fuel their movements. In its purest sense, Jihad is a peaceful, noble, internal pursuit of wholesomeness. In the extremist context, it expands the concept of struggle to take an outward manifestation of violence to achieve its ends.[35] It is in this context that the

Jihadist ends align with the ways (terror tactics) to manifest violence as the means to

overcome the struggle. Jihad in and of itself is not terrorism, but terror is the preferred

tactic of the Jihadist.

Al Qaeda plays a leading role in a larger political and military movement called

"global jihad." Global jihad is an extremist splinter group within Islamism, a broad

religious movement that seeks to instill a stricter observance in politics, economics, and

society. [36] Al Qaeda has codified their objectives into long and short-term goals.

> "the movement has a number of short-term aims including the eviction of
> foreign forces from the Islamic world, and the termination of corrupt and
> pro-Western regimes in countries such as Saudi Arabia, Egypt, and
> Pakistan and a number of others that form a cluster termed "the near
> enemy". They also bitterly oppose the state of Israel. All of these are
> short-term goals, but still measured in decades rather than years – much
> longer than typical Western political timescales."[37]

For Al Qaeda, the ultimate long term goal is the establishment of a new state, or

global caliphate.[38] The political and physical form of the caliphate starts with a

collection of like minded Islamic emirates, or mini-states that are not necessarily

organized under one leader or government. This forms the basis for the true Islamic

caliphate, a single political entity governed as the Prophet guided the early Muslim

peoples.[39] Extremists view the U.S. policy of promoting democracy in the Muslim world

as another assault on Islam. Global jihadis oppose secularism in any form: democracy,

nationalism, communism, and any other un-Islamic system or philosophy.[40] The

establishment of a caliphate is a goal requiring generations of struggle and it also pits

the Muslim world against the non-Muslim world. For this reason, some believe the

Muslim world to be at war with the West, which is as inaccurate and distorted as equating the GWOT to a war against Islam. The majority of Muslims do not support Al Qaeda and Islamic extremists are in the minority.[41] In fact, a Gallup World Poll found that,

> "both politically radicalized and moderate Muslims admire the West"s fair political systems - democracy, respect of human rights, freedom of speech, and gender equality. Looking at their own countries, a significantly higher percentage of the politically radicalized (50 percent versus 35 percent of moderates), contrary to popular belief, say that "moving toward greater governmental democracy" will foster progress in the Arab/Muslim world." [42]

This research indicates that extremists, in zeal to pursue their agendas, are also guilty of failing to understand the environment and address the underlying causes of a frustrated, angry, and marginalized people from whom they hope to draw support. One of the complexities of extremism is that many of the terrorists are drawn from the resident population they seek to assail. Among the many advantages this affords, it enables groups like Al Qaeda and the Taliban to melt away into society to avoid military defeat.[43] This phenomenon also presents flaws in the extremist movement that the U.S. has yet to fully exploit. Radical ideologue Abu Bakr Naji raised concerns about clerics challenging the legitimacy of the movement and siphoning off recruits, excessive use of force against fellow Muslims, and similar to the 9-11 attack, targeting the wrong people at the wrong time would turn the masses away from the movement.[44] Al Qaeda associate Abu Mus ab al-Suri, an astute observer of Western strategic thinking, worried that jihad had failed in the past because it ignored ethnic minorities, failed to keep clerics involved, and propaganda threatened the legitimacy of the jihad movement.[45]

In his call for "holy war," Osama Bin Laden has argued that the Muslim world was subject to aggression from a host of enemies to include Jews, crusaders, Western society and the "apostate" governments of the Arab world. His dictum for the violent emancipation of Muslims all over the world knows no boundaries.[46] Extremists, in declaring "jihad" against all that do not practice their militant beliefs have united these disparate enemies against them. Just as the specter of a GWOT created a polarizing consequence, the rhetoric of militant jihad casts the enemy as a broad cooperative entity. This effect has unified disparate parties and provided them with a cohesive purpose to oppose extremism with the combined might of their assets and collective will.

Recommendations for a New Course

An effective U.S. counterterrorism effort should begin with more enlightened thinking to understand the multi-dimensional complexities of the environment. New policies and strategies ought to shape the environment over generations rather than reacting to it in the near-term. Addressing the wider global issues has greater effect in countering terrorism than wielding military might to crush it as it materializes. The instruments of national power have been applied disproportionately to the problem and must be brought into balance in order to undercut support for extremism and provide viable solutions.

In attempting to determine the nature, cause and sources of the terrorist threat, the U.S. has been hampered by binary thinking,

> "Western thought views things as black or white, good or evil and us and them. Thinking of terrorism simply as evil does not provide a useful understanding of the enemy and this vagueness blurs the strategy. Thinking in terms of complementary opposites, for example, there is no day without night better illustrates the yin and yang of concepts that are not separate, but are two parts to make a unified whole... defining radical Islam as an ideology of hate is a binary view that implies that extremists can only explained as the opposite of peaceful, loving and law abiding.

This obstructs an understanding of why Muslims would sympathize or support Al Qaeda... an ideology that appeals to things they value most – God, Islam, their brethren, justice and honor."[47]

Appreciating the duality in the nature of the problem is important in stemming the tide of extremism. Resentment of the West or the pursuit of religious purity does not make one a terrorist. They represent but a few layers of underlying causes that must be understood and addressed to prevent adoption or support of terrorism. Policies should seek a middle ground, not an either-or type of solution. The Palestinian problem has long been a lightning rod of Muslim-Western tension, with the U.S. being more sympathetic toward Israel at the expense of Arab states. A more moderate stance on the Arab-Israeli conflict is paramount to improved Muslim relations with the West and channeling the anger and humiliation it inspires into more constructive discourse. Notably, the U.S. has played a significant role in Middle-Eastern politics, and as a major actor, is held liable for political defects.[48] Aggressive multi-lateral engagement encouraging Middle-Eastern governments to enact progressive reform is necessary to reduce the political repression, and ameliorate the stigma of democratic exceptionalism to enhance America"s image. There is also a need to push the jihadists into defending themselves, and answer the question of what precisely they have done of late to help solve the problems of Iraq, Afghanistan, or Pakistan. Keeping the pressure on in this way could go a long way toward publicizing the Islamists" lack of vision.[49]

Terrorism is not a new phenomenon; if it was born as a last resort instrument of politics for the out-group, then creating new political outlets for terrorist groups may possibly assuage them. Offering political alternatives as part of a containment policy makes terrorist acts less attractive and potentially forces terrorism into a dormant state.[50] As the U.S. seeks international cooperation to advance its security agenda, a shift from preemption towards containment is likely more accepted and falls well within the norms of international law and consequently generates greater support.[51]

Regardless of the motivation or justification of the U.S. incursions into Afghanistan and Iraq, those wars have global implications and must be fought on their own merit to national strategic objectives. Each represents regional security and foreign policy interests and do in fact play a part in combating terrorism. Abandonment or defeat would provide a tremendous boost to extremist worldwide and leave the region vulnerable to chaos. Neither conflict provides an avenue to strike a decisive blow against terrorism; however, successful outcomes may result in local stability and improved security in one of the world"s most volatile regions. U.S. victory is more readily attained if those wars are de-linked from a fight against terrorism and proceed with strategies to defeat the adversary they are engaged with. The U.S. and its allies need to pursue those operations for what they truly are; counterinsurgencies to establish governance and stability in a region of vital strategic importance to national and global interests.

Combating terrorism is like eating an elephant - it can be done, one bite at a time. It requires patience and singular purpose. A war against terror is like trying to eat a stampede; the infeasibility of the task invites the risk of being trampled by the herd. Like the metaphorical stampede, the "war on terror" can no longer be perceived as the war to eradicate terror. Terrorism can be limited, but it cannot be eliminated by force.[52] The U.S. can, however, contain terrorism through a comprehensive national strategy that leverages all aspects of U.S. power; and where necessary, that of its regional allies and partners. Policy should inform strategy and both must address the long term threat, which is measured in decades and generations, not in years. Focusing on root causes that inspire terrorist movements enables policy makers and strategists to evaluate the environment more clearly and accurately.

Terrorists have agendas designed to meet their objectives. Terrorists seek to influence policy or political outcomes in terms that are favorable to their interests. Terror is the tactic, it is not the agenda. Effective strategies neutralize the agenda rather than the tactic, by addressing underlying causes that create marginalized societies. If those root causes are not addressed, the disenfranchised Muslim populations of Europe or Africa may present the next challenge. A policy of containment offers a greater chance for success and is more likely to secure international consensus than war. Policy backed by deeds, has the potential to reduce anti-Western sentiment and improve foreign relations.

Acknowledging the distinction between the institution and practices of Islam from the radicals that practice terrorism increases the potential for cooperation and partnership between the West and the nearly two billion Muslims in the world. A smaller military footprint and the lack of spectacular battles to rally the public against would cripple the recruiting and radicalization efforts of extremists. It also frustrates the primary purpose of local jihad, which is not the overthrow of the West, but the training and indoctrination of the rising generation of jihadis.[53]

Reframing the problem reveals that containment applies a better balance of all instruments of national power in a more effective manner than a military-centric solution, and is sustainable over a longer period of time. Containment will not defeat Al Qaeda, neither will the current strategy. A containment policy is more in line with the art of the

possible, which is the component that strategy provides to policy. After ten years on the

offensive against terrorism, extremists still plan and attempt attacks against the U.S. It

is time to address the reasons why they try.

Endnotes

[1] Ronald W. Reagan, *National Security Decision Directive (NSDD) -179*, (Washington, DC: The White House, July 17, 1985), http://www.fas.org/irp/offdocs/nsdd/23-2628a.gif (accessed November 3, 2010).

[2] Terrorism Project. (*Chronology of Major Terrorist Attacks Against US Targets*, (Center for Defense Information, n.d.) http://www.cdi.org/terrorism/chronology.html (accessed November 1, 2010).

[3] William J. Clinton, *Presidential Decision Directive (PDD) – 39*, , (Washington, DC: The White House, June 21, 1995), http://www.fas.org/irp/offdocs/pdd/pdd-39.pdf (accessed November 3, 2010).

[4] Executive Order 13228 of October 8, 2001, *Establishing the Office of Homeland Security and the Homeland Security Council*, (The Federal Register, Vol. 66, No. 196, Washington, DC, October 10, 2001), http://frwebgate.access.gpo.gov/cgibin/getdoc.cgi?dbname=2001_register&docid=fr10oc01-144.pdf , (accessed November 2, 2010).

[5] Glenn Kessler and Peter Baker, Bush"s *"Axis of Evil" Comes Back to Haunt United States*, Washington Post, October 10, 2006. http://www.washingtonpost.com/wp-dyn/content/article/2006/10/09/AR2006100901130.html , (accessed November 3, 2010).

[6] Thomas Donnelly, *The Underpinnings of the Bush Doctrine*, (American Enterprise Institute for Public Policy Research Series, February 2003), http://www.aei.org/outlook/15845 , (accessed February 15, 2011).

[7] Barrack H. Obama, *Remarks to the Nation on the Way Forward in Afghanistan and Pakistan*, (US Military Academy at West Point, December 1, 2009), http://www.whitehouse.gov/the-press-office/remarks-president-address-nation-way-forward-afghanistan-and-pakistan# (accessed November 5, 2010).

[8] Sarah E. Zabel *The Military Strategy of Global Jihad*. Carlisle Barracks: US Army War College, Strategic Studies Institute, October 2007. 18pp. (U413 .C2Z11 2007) http://www.strategicstudiesinstitute.army.mil/pubs/download.cfm?q=809 , (accessed November 5, 2010).

[9] Title 22 United States Code, section 2656f(d), Annual Country Reports on Terrorism. http://www.law.cornell.edu/uscode/422/usc_sec_22_00002656---f000-.html (accessed November 5, 2010).

[10] Joint Publication 1-02, *DOD Dictionary of Military and Associated Terms,* 12 April 2001, (as amended through 30 September 2010), 468.

[11] Straight UN Facts, *Eye on the UN*, a project of the Hudson Institute, New York, http://www.eyeontheun.org/facts.asp?1=1&p=61 , (accessed December 17, 2010).

[12] "UN Reform". United Nations. 2005-03-21. Archived from the original on 2007-04-27. http://web.archive.org/web/20070427012107/http://www.un.org/unifeed/script.asp?scriptId=73. Retrieved 2008-07-11. "The second part of the report, entitled "Freedom from Fear backs the definition of terrorism–an issue so divisive agreement on it has long eluded the world community–as any action "intended to cause death or serious bodily harm to civilians or non-combatants with the purpose of intimidating a population or compelling a government or an international organization to do or abstain from doing any act""

[13] Free Online Encyclopedia, http://encyclopedia2.thefreedictionary.com/War , (accessed December 17, 2010).

[14] Gilles Andreani, *The "War on Terror": Good Cause, Wrong Concept* , Survival*, vol 46, no 4, Winter 2004-05 pp. 31-50: 31.

[15] Ruba Ali, *The Bush Administration and the Problem of Torture*, n.p., August 2005, http://www.osgoode.yorku.ca/glsa/2007conference/documents/Ruba%20Ali%20-%20The%20Bush%20Administration%20and%20the%20Problem%20of%20Torture.pdf , (accessed December 21, 2010).

[16] Paul Rogers, *Why We're Losing the War on Terror*. Malden, MA: Polity, 2008. 119.

[17] Davis Allsop, *The Viability of Deterring Terrorism*, June 11, 2010. http://www.e-ir.info/?p=4330#_ftn2 (accessed December 28, 2010).

[18] N.I. Klonis, *Guerrilla Warfare: Analysis and Projections* (New York: Robert Speller, 1972) 5-6.

[19] M.L.R. Smith, *Guerrillas in the Mist: Reassessing Strategy and Low Intensity Warfare*, Review of International Studies, Vol. 29, No. 1 (2003), 20.

[20] Andreani, *"The "War on Terror,"* 39.

[21] Steven R. Watt, *Can the United States "Defeat" Al Qaeda?,* Strategy Research Project (Carlisle Barracks, PA: U.S. Army War College, March 19, 2010), 18.

[22] Harry R. Yarger, *Strategic Theory for the 21st Century: The Little Big Book on Big Strategy,* The Letort Papers, US Army War College, February 2006.

[23] Carl von Clausewitz, *On War*, Edited and translated by Michael Howard and Peter Paret (Princeton, New Jersey: Princeton University Press, 1976), 88.

[24] Scott Wilson and Al Kamen, *"Global War on Terror" is Given a New Name*, Washington Post, March 25, 2009.

[25] Ibid.

[26] For definitions based on terrorism as a form of violence against the "innocent" see Christopher C. Harmon, *Terrorism Today* (London: Frank Cass, 2000), p. 21; Jessica Stern, *The Ultimate Terrorists* (Cambridge, MA: Harvard University Press, 1999), 11.

[27] Peter R. Neuman and M.L.R. Smith, *The Strategy of Terrorism, How it Works and Why it Fails*, Contemporary Terrorism Studies, (Routledge, New York, N.Y., 2008), 8.

[28] Joshua Sinai, A Conceptual Framework for Resolving Terrorism"s Root Causes, in *Root Causes of Terrorism: Myths, Reality and the Ways Forward*, ed. By Tore Bjorgo,(Routledge, New York, NY, 2005), 215.

[29] Ibid, 21.

[30] John L. Esposito and Dalia Mogahed, *Battle for Muslims' Hearts and Minds: The Road Not (Yet) Taken,* Middle East Policy, Washington: Spring 2007. Vol. 14, Iss. 1; 27.

[31] Jacquelyn K. Davis, and Charles M. Perry. *Rethinking the War on Terror: Developing a Strategy to Counter Extremist Ideologies: A Workshop Report*. Washington, DC: (Institute for Foreign Policy Analysis, March 2007. 20pp., 2007), I. http://www.ifpa.org/pdf/Rethink_WOT.pdf (accessed December 17, 2010).

[32] Brachman, Jarret M., and William F. McCants. *Stealing Al-Qa'ida's Playbook*. West Point: USMilitary Academy, Combating Terrorism Center, February 2006. 25pp. (2006), 18. http://ctc.usma.edu/pdf/Stealing%20Al-Qai'da's%20Playbook%20--%20CTC.pdf (accessed December 17, 2010).

[33] Esposito and Mogahed, "Battle for Muslims" Hearts and Minds," 27.

[34] Davis and Perry, "Rethinking the War on Terror". I.

[35] Michael G. Knapp, "The Concept and Practice of Jihad in Islam*," Parameters*, (Spring 2003), 82. http://www.carlisle.army.mil/USAWC/parameters/Articles/03spring/knapp.pdf (accessed January 16, 2011).

[36] Sarah E. Zabel, *The Military Strategy of Global Jihad*. Carlisle Barracks: U.S. Army War College, (Strategic Studies Institute, October 2007). 1. http://www.strategicstudiesinstitute.army.mil/pubs/download.cfm?q=809 (accessed December 17, 2010).

[37] Paul Rogers,"Reconsidering the War on Terror," *RUSI Journal*, vol.152, no. 4 (August 2007), 33.

[38] The caliphate is a single Muslim state operated as the Prophet did the first Muslim state. "Caliph" means "successor" in Arabic; the caliph is the successor to the Prophet in that he guides the people of Earth to live in accordance with God"s laws in all respects: politically,

economically, and socially, as well as religiously. The caliphate is the physical and political form of government over the lands and peoples the caliph guides.

[39] Zabel, "The Military Strategy of Global Jihad," 4.

[40] Ibid, 3.

[41] In mid-2005 and early 2006, the Gallup Organization surveyed 10 predominantly Muslim countries (Morocco, Egypt, Turkey, Lebanon, Jordan, Saudi Arabia, Iran, Pakistan, Indonesia and Bangladesh) as part of its new World Poll, which by the end of 2006 will survey about 130 countries, including more than 35 that are predominantly Muslim. There were 1,000 in-home, face-to-face surveys per country, with sampling in urban and rural areas that is the statistical equivalent of surveying the nation's adult population, with a statistical-sampling error rate of plus or minus 3 percentage points.

The findings of the Gallup World Poll provide a critical foundation and context for understanding the nature and origins of radical views, as well as perceptions about Western attempts to foster democratic governments.

To determine who might be accurately categorized as "politically radicalized" and (moderate," Gallup looked at how respondents answered a question about the moral justification of the 9/11 attacks and their favorability ratings of the United States. Those who said the 9/11 attacks were completely morally justified and who also have an unfavorable or very unfavorable opinion of the United States were termed politically radicalized and thus potential supporters of terrorism. Those who did not say the attacks were completely justified were termed moderates. This group of "moderates" can be further broken down into "skeptical moderates," those with unfavorable opinions of the United States (51 percent), and "pro-U.S. moderates," those with neutral to favorable opinions of the United States (38 percent).

[42] Esposito and Mogahed, "Battle for Muslims" Hearts and Minds," 27.

[43] Paul Rogers,"Reconsidering the War on Terror," *RUSI Journal*, vol.152, no. 4 (August 2007), 33.

[44] Brachman and McCants. "Stealing Al-Qa'ida's Playbook," 9.

[45] Ibid, 17.

[46] Andreani, *The "War on Terror,"* 36.

[47] Charles Pena, *Winning the Un-War: A New Strategy for the War on Terrorism*, (Potomac Books, Inc. Washington, D.C., 2006), 97-118.

[48] Abdullah Yousef Sahar Mohammad, Roots of Terrorism in the Middle East, in *Root Causes of Terrorism: Myths, Reality and the Ways Forward*, ed. By Tore Bjorgo,(Routledge, New York, NY, 2005), 116.

[49] Davis and Perry, "Rethinking the War on Terror". III.

[50] Allsop, "The Viability of Deterring Terrorism."

[51] Norman M. Worthen, Retooling Deterrence for the Long War, Strategy Research Project (Carlisle Barracks, PA: U.S. Army War College, March 15, 2008), 17.

[52] Ibid

[53] Brachman and McCants. "Stealing Al-Qa'ida's Playbook," 17.